Contents

Any words appearing in the text in bold, **like this**, are explained in the glossary.

Information all around us

You are surrounded by information.
Information is what people know about things.
Information can be signs, pictures, or words
that tell you how to do things or where to go.

 Information can be found in books
and newspapers, on the Internet,
and through asking questions.

In your everyday life you often need to choose information from different **sources**. This book will help you to find out which information you need, whatever you are doing.

 Always be prepared to ask for help.

How do I choose?

The best way of choosing which **source** of information to use depends on what you want the information for. For example, you might want to find out where your nearest football club plays. Doing a search on the Internet should help you find the answer.

 You could also do a search using a mobile phone.

If you have a new pet, you probably want to find out how to look after it properly. You will have to work out which sources will provide the information you need. In this case, the Internet, books, and your vet will be good sources of information.

A library is a good place to look for information.

Understand the question

If you are choosing information for a school **project**, then the first thing to do is to make sure you understand the question. Make a list of what you already know about the topic. What do you need to find out?

 If you are not sure exactly which are the best **sources** to use, ask your teacher or librarian to help you.

An **encyclopedia** can be a good place to start. If you need more precise information, you can look in other **reference books**. If you are not sure what you are looking for, go back to your question. Make a list of possible **keywords** for an Internet search.

 A print or **online** encyclopedia will give you general background information and an overview of the topic.

Which information can we trust?

You can trust some **sources** more than others. This is because **facts** can get confused with **opinion**. Facts are what people know for sure about a topic. Facts are the same in different sources. Opinions are the feelings of one person or one group of people about a topic. Opinions cannot be proven.

 This boy has an opinion about carrots.

It is always good to read information for yourself, so that you know you can trust it.

You should also be careful about trusting information that comes directly from people. Someone may tell you something that they have heard or read, but you cannot always be sure that what they have told you is correct. People can twist the facts to match their opinions, or they may not understand your question.

11

When will we land on the moon?

A _____

4

 Is this book up-to-date?

Books are one of the most reliable **sources** of information. This is because they are usually carefully checked before they are **published**. **Experts** read the information inside books to make sure it is correct.

It is best to use websites that have been created by a well-known organization or by the government. If you are not sure whether a website is useful, you can check with a teacher or librarian.

 Lots of information can be found on the Internet, but not all of it can be trusted.

Understanding information

During your search, you may come across information that is difficult to understand. This could be because it was written for older children or adults. Sometimes you can ask an adult to help you understand, but it is better to try to find **sources** aimed at your own age group.

Ask for help if you don't understand something.

If you are not sure the information you found is useful, try a simple test. Can you explain the information to a friend or classmate in your own words? If it seems too difficult then try another source.

Try to use sources of information that are the right level for your age group.

Too much information!

 When you use the Internet it is easy to start looking at information you do not need. Try to stay focused on what you really need to find.

Sometimes it is difficult to organize the information you have found because there is so much of it. You must take only what you need from the **sources** of information you have found.

Look back at your **project** or your question. Sort out the information that answers your question and completes your project. Get rid of the information that does not.

 Talk to friends about the information they have found.

A range of information

When you use a range of **sources**, you can **cross-check** the **facts**. This means that if you find a fact in one source and then find the same information in a different source, the fact is more likely to be correct.

 Some people believe that you should find the same information in three sources before you can be sure that it is correct.

When you look at a number of different sources, you need to be careful not to copy other people's work. Copying is stealing the work of another person. You should always put the information you find into your own words.

 Find information from different sources and then put it into your own words.

Keep a record

You should always keep a record of the different **sources** you use when you search for information. Your record of sources will show your teacher that you have found facts. Your record can also tell others where to look to learn more about your topic.

 A librarian can help you find a source. He or she can also help you keep a record of your source.

It is a good idea to keep a list of useful information sources in case you want to use them again.

Your teacher may ask you to list the sources you have used at the end of a piece of schoolwork. Then your teacher can see what research you have done. It is also a way of thanking the person or group who provided the information for you.

What comes next?

Some information is good to share out loud.

The best **sources** of information will depend on the type of information you are looking for. It will also depend on how you plan to use the information. Be aware of how you can trust some sources more than others.

Sorting out the information you have found can be hard work. However, once you have chosen the information you want to keep, the next step is to work out how to use it.

 Information can be found in so many places it can be confusing.

Activities

Making a tourist leaflet

Imagine a tourist is coming to visit your area. Design an information leaflet about where you live. Try finding three or four different **sources** of information. Choose the most useful information from each of the sources. Put the **facts** together into a leaflet and do not forget to include pictures.

You could take photographs of a member of your family, your pet, or your favourite toy.

Taking photographs for a poster

Use a digital camera to take some photographs. Then use a computer to look at the pictures and choose the best two or three to use. Make a poster of your pictures. Write two sentences about each photograph you have chosen.

Glossary

advert made by companies to get people to buy the DVDs, toys, or other things they make. Information in adverts is usually one-sided.

cross-check checking a particular piece of information in a number of sources

encyclopedia book with information about many subjects, or on a particular subject

expert person who has a lot of knowledge about a particular topic

fact something that is known for certain about a topic

imprint page page in a book which gives information about who helped to create the book and when it was written. An imprint page usually appears near the beginning of a book.

keyword word that describes the particular subject you want to find information about

online connected to the Internet

opinion thoughts and feelings about a topic that one person or group of people may have

project task set by a teacher that can be done on your own or with other people

published printed materials, such as books and magazines, produced for sale

reference book a book, such as a dictionary or encyclopaedia, that you can use to find reliable information

source place in which we can find information. Books, television, and the Internet are sources of information.

Find out more

Books

My First Email Guide, Chris Oxlade (Heinemann Library, 2007)

My First Internet Guide, Chris Oxlade (Heinemann Library, 2007)

Websites

Yahoo! Kids – Homework Help
http://kids.yahoo.com/learn
This website includes links to an encyclopedia, dictionary, maps, and lots of other useful websites.

CBBC Newsround
http://www.bbc.co.uk/cbbc/help/safesurfing
This BBC website gives you advice on staying safe while you are on the Internet.

Index